Find Your Future in Science

Diane Lindsey Reeves

Created and produced by
Bright Futures Press, Cary, North Carolina
www.brightfuturespress.com

Published by
Cherry Lake Publishing, Ann Arbor, Michigan
www.cherrylakepublishing.com

Photo Credits: page 4 (top), ©Shutterstock/shebeko; page 4 (left), ©Shutterstock/vladgrin; page 6 (top), ©Shutterstock/agsandrew; page 6 (left), ©Shutterstock/leyaarts; page 7, ©Shutterstock/Real Illusion; page 8, ©Shutterstock/Baldas1950; page 9 (top), ©Shutterstock/isak55; page 9 (left), ©Shutterstock/R Gino Santa Maria; page 10, ©Shutterstock/studiowoodo; page 10, ©Shutterstock/djem; page 11, ©Shutterstock/studioVin; page 12 (top), ©Shutterstock/ASE; page 12 (left), ©Shutterstock/CHOATphotographer; page 13, ©Shutterstock/juliann; page 14, ©Shutterstock/Gwoeii; page 15 (top), ©Shutterstock/FikMik; page 15 (left), Kelvin Wong; page 16, ©Shutterstock/The Turtle Factory; page 17, ©Shutterstock/06photo; page 18 (top), ©Shutterstock/Fer Gregory; page 18 (left) Yuri Samsonov; page 18, ©Shutterstock/Lecter; page 20, ©Shutterstock/Digital Storm; page 21 (top), ©Shutterstock/Willyam Bradberry; page 21 (left), ©Shutterstock/Africa Studio; page 22, ©Shutterstock/new4a; page 23, ©Shutterstock/Kekyalyaynen; page 24 (top), ©Shutterstock/Andrea Izzotti; page 24 (left), ©Shutterstock/dedpixto; page 25, ©Shutterstock/angkrit; page 26, ©Shutterstock/stockphoto_graf; page 27 (top), ©Shutterstock/Jeng Niamwahnl55; page 26(left), ©Shutterstock/Volodymyr Krasyuk; page 28, ©Shutterstock/TeddyandMia; page 28, ©Shutterstock/Aleutie; page 29, ©Shutterstock/Tyler Olson.

Library of Congress Cataloging-in-Publication Date

Names: Reeves, Diane Lindsey, 1959- author.
Title: Find your future in science / by Diane Lindsey Reeves.
Description: Ann Arbor, Michigan: Cherry Lake Publishing, [2016] | Series: Find Your Future in STEAM | Audience: Grades 4 to 6. | Includes index.
Identifiers: LCCN 2016006585| ISBN 9781634718981 (hardcover) | ISBN 9781634719445 (pbk.) | ISBN 9781634719216 (pdf) | ISBN 9781634719674 (ebook)
Subjects: LCSH: Science--Vocational guidance--Juvenile literature. | CYAC: Vocational guidance.
Classification: LCC Q147 .R377 2016 | DDC 502.3--dc23
LC record available at http://lccn.loc.gov/2016006585

Printed in the United States of America.

Table of Contents

Find Your Future in Science

Find your future in science

Scientists start out as curious kids, a lot like you. They find something that really interests them. It might be worms. It might be rocks. It might be a fascination with black holes in outer space.

Whatever sparks a connection.

Young scientists start asking lots of questions. *Why? How? What if?*

Curiosity keeps them exploring. Every fascinating discovery lights a spark, an idea, an interest, a connection!

Before they know it, they are hooked. Science is awesome!

Then they find out they can grow up and be a scientist. What? You mean that companies will actually pay you to do science as your job? Yes, scientists can do what they love and make a living too. How cool is that?

This book—and other titles in the *Find Your Future* series—is especially for kids who really like science. It's also for kids who collect rocks or bugs, love nature hikes, and ask lots of questions about everything. Either way, read on to find out some amazing things scientists do.

Find a science career that interests you, and...

Surf the 'Net!

Type the words that are **bold** in the Surf the 'Net sections of this book into your favorite Internet search engine (like Google, Bing, or Yahoo) to find more information about the subject. Be sure to have permission and SUPERVISION from a trusted adult (like a teacher or parent) when going online.

Explore Some More!

In this book you'll find ideas you can use to explore cool resources in websites, in the news, and in fun online games. Here's your chance to goof around and learn some more.

Ask Big Questions!

Curiosity opens the door to learning (and fun!). Ponder the questions posed here. Each question comes with an activity you can do. Use them to share your answers through posters, games, presentations, or even a good discussion where you consider both sides of an idea.

Go online to download free activity sheets at www.cherrylakepublishing.com/activities.

Astrophysicist

Surf the 'Net!

Get acquainted with some of history's most famous stargazers. What did Galileo Galilei, Sir Isaac Newton, Albert Einstein, and Edwin Hubble discover?

Want to know how many stars there are? Count every grain of sand on Earth. It's just a guess, but that's how many stars some people say are out there in our **galaxy**.

Powerful **telescopes**, like the Hubble Space Telescope operated by NASA, have revealed more than 170 billion galaxies. That means there could actually be 1,000,000,000,000,000,000,000,000 planets out there! (That's one **septillion**, in case you are counting.) All are waiting to be discovered, explored, and searched for signs of life.

Astronomy is the study of the universe—its stars, planets, galaxies, dark matter, and energy. Everything out there is of interest to astronomers down here. **Physics** is the science that looks at matter, energy, motion, and force. Put astronomy and physics together, and you get astrophysics—and the makings of an out-of-this-world career.

Astrophysics is an ancient science. Scientists have been gazing at stars, naming them, and watching for changes for centuries. Even so, there is still much to be learned. **Astrophysicists** at colleges, government agencies, and really cool space observatories continue to keep an eye on the skies, using tools that early stargazers never imagined.

These researchers continue to make amazing discoveries. In recent years scientists downgraded Pluto's status from a planet to a dwarf planet. They found a black hole in the center of our Milky Way.

Ask Big Questions!

Imagine a friendly visitor from outer space has landed in your backyard. It wants to know more about Earth. Once you figure out how to communicate with space aliens... **What can you tell them about the planet you call home?** Write a letter to the alien telling it what life is like here on Earth.

Explore Some More!

Visit the NASA Kids' Club at **www.nasa.gov/audience/forkids/home.**

And they proved a way to determine a star's age by the speed of its spin. Their work helps us better understand the universe and how we earthlings fit into it.

Other astrophysicists work in ways that apply knowledge about the universe in practical ways. For instance, some astrophysicists work for companies that build and monitor **satellites**. They use these to observe the earth for potential disasters or monitor climate change.

Reach for the stars as an astrophysicist, and someday you might work (and even live!) on the moon or Mars. Who knows? You might be the first person to discover life on another planet.

One of the millions of space photographs taken by the Hubble telescope. This one is of the Sombero Galaxy, 28 million light years from Earth. It has 800 billion suns and is 50,000 light years wide.

Chemist

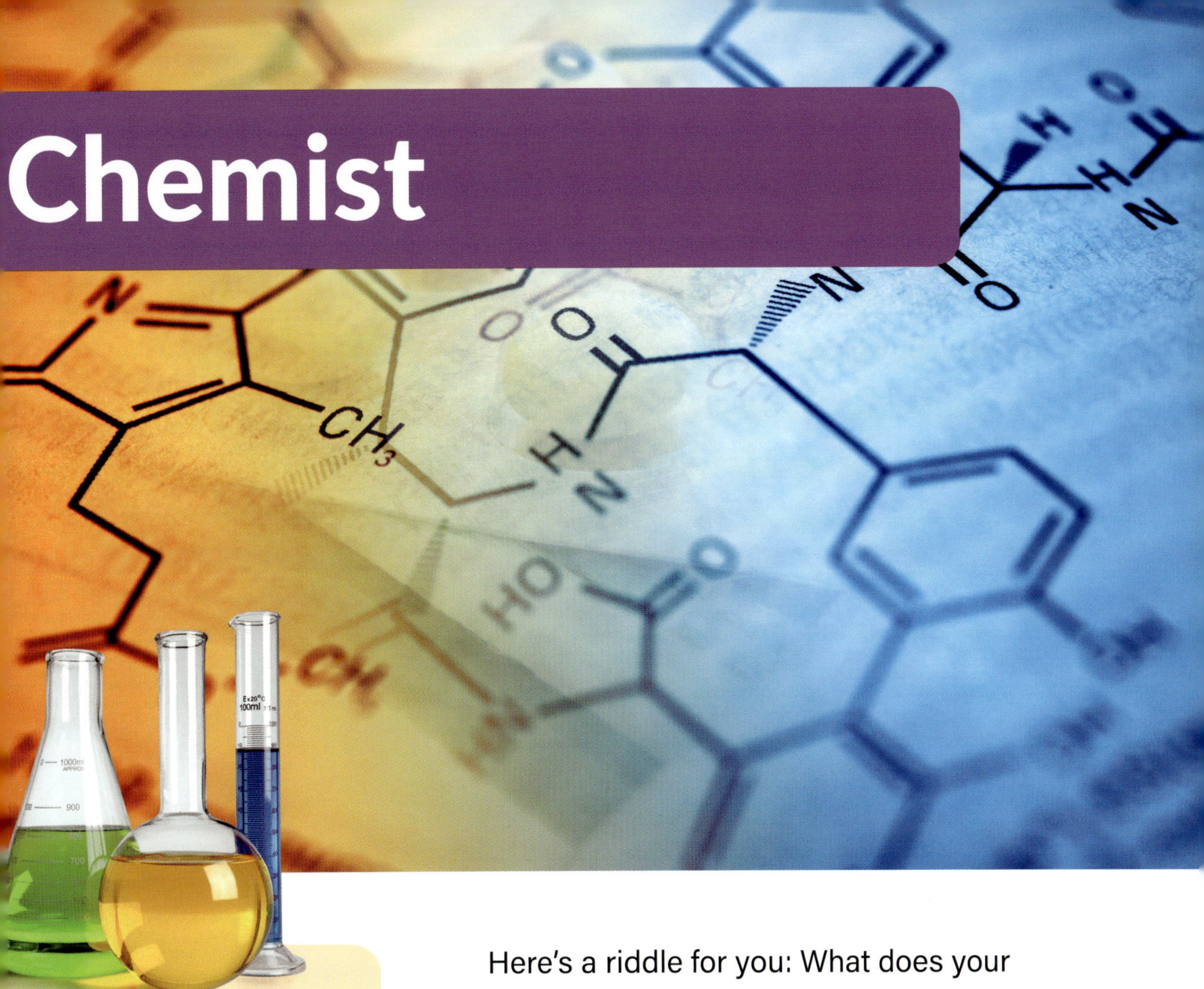

Surf the 'Net!

Search the Internet for the **Periodic Table Song**, for a fun way to memorize the periodic table of elements.

Here's a riddle for you: What does your body have in common with a cell phone, a hockey puck, and a bag of jelly beans? They are all made of chemicals!

Chemists are scientists who put chemicals together in ways that solve problems or create products. The results of their work can save lives or make the world a better place. Think curing cancer or earth-friendly fuel sources. Some chemists work to solve simple, everyday problems, like inventing deodorants that pass the stink test after recess on a sunny day.

According to the American Chemical Society, humans have found or made more than 50 million unique chemicals. That's a lot of chemicals! Which is one reason chemists tend to specialize in certain types of products or processes.

For instance, pharmaceutical companies research, develop, and manufacture all kinds of medicines. Other chemists develop products with metals, ceramics, rubber, adhesives, and paints.

Agricultural chemists develop safe herbicides and insecticides. Lots of chemists work in the food industry, testing for the Food and Drug Administration (FDA) or coming up with new stuff like sodas or snacks. They work for companies that manufacture gasoline for cars, as well as those that produce oils, lubricants, fabrics, fibers, or even explosives.

You might not realize that chemists are involved in developing cosmetics and

Ask Big Questions!

Everything, including you, is made of chemicals. In fact, 99 percent of your body is composed of six elements. **What six elements is the human body composed of?** Make an outline of the human body and "decorate" it with the names of these elements.

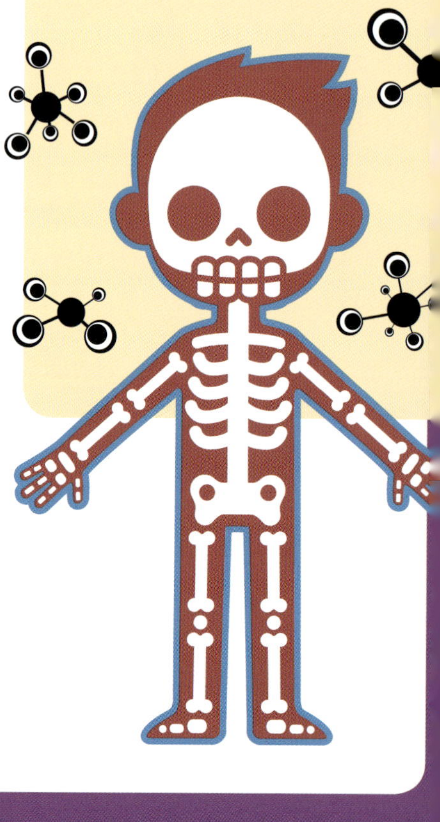

fragrances too. Chemists also come up with new and improved formulas for bathroom tissue, soaps, and detergents. Browse the aisle at your local supermarket and you'll see that chemists stay busy creating all kinds of options. There are beauty products promising to solve any problem!

Sometimes chemicals solve one problem but cause another one. This is true of certain metals and solvents used in manufacturing. They cause pollution. So do some pesticides used in farming. They can also cause health problems in humans and animals.

Making safer, earth-friendly chemicals is a big challenge waiting for future chemists.

Explore Some More!

Get ready for some adventures in chemistry with the American Chemical Society at **www.acs.org/content/acs/en/education/whatischemistry/adventures-in-chemistry.html**.

Everyday household products—and their plastic containers—all have chemists behind them.

Crime Scene Investigator

Surf the 'Net!

Track down clues about the **history of fingerprints**.

If you have ever watched a detective show on television, you might have seen some of the characters processing a crime scene. Crime scene investigators (CSI) are forensic scientists who carefully gather evidence. You'll see them taking photographs and filling evidence bags.

Real crime scene investigators don't solve crimes in an hour (minus commercials). But like those on TV, CSIs approach a crime scene as if it were a giant puzzle. Their job is put all the pieces together to help prove whodunit.

What do crime scene investigators look for? It depends on the type of crime and how it was committed. Fingerprints and other sources of human **DNA**, like hair and blood, are high on the list. Fingerprints and DNA are unique to each person. When a criminal leaves this type of evidence behind, it's almost like they left a big sign that says "I did it."

Clues can be found in the weirdest places. Say the criminal leaves behind a big wad of chewing gum. Not only can crime scene investigators test it for DNA, they can also match dental impressions to a suspect's teeth. A lipstick smear might be matched to a tube found in a suspect's purse. Every clue counts!

Forensic scientists use all kinds of amazing equipment to examine each piece of evidence. Fingerprints are run through a national database program to look for hits with known criminals. Or they

Ask Big Questions!

How does DNA evidence work in solving crimes? Pluck a single hair from your head and examine it under a microscope or magnifying glass. Compare your hair with a hair from a friend or family member. Jot down notes of the similarities and differences.

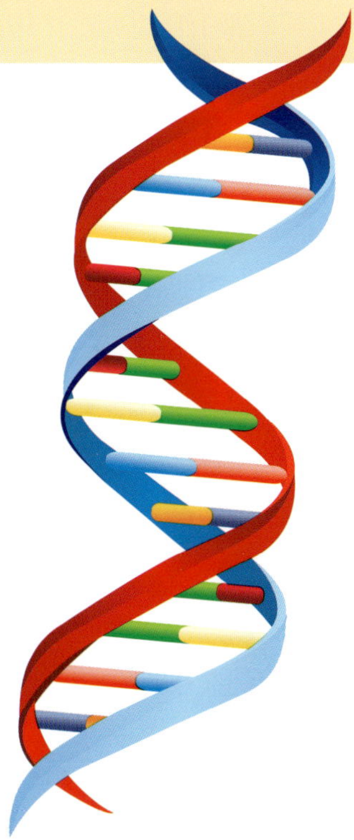

Explore Some More!

Tag along for some CSI Web Adventures at **forensics.rice.edu**.

run tests to see if the fingerprints match those of specific suspects in the case.

Ditto for DNA. CSIs can run DNA tests on the tiniest bits of human matter—a strand of hair, a droplet of blood, saliva on the back of a postage stamp. DNA often provides conclusive evidence in a case because DNA does not lie!

Firearms, footprints, tire tracks, fabrics, and even computer and cell phone files are also analyzed as possible evidence. You never know which clues will crack the case!

Thanks to the work of forensic scientists, many a criminal has learned that crime doesn't pay.

Clues to solve crimes can be found in all kinds of evidence.

Environmental Scientist

Surf the 'Net!

Ecology and **kids** make a great match, so find out what cool stuff you can discover about the planet we call home.

Well-informed citizen that you are, you probably know the environment is a big deal. There is a lot of talk about being earth-friendly, going green, and finding **sustainable** solutions.

Environmental scientists need to understand how the earth works and how it supports life. They need to find ways for humans to, um, be human and enjoy their basic rights of "life, liberty, and the pursuit of happiness" without messing up the earth. Environmental scientists have very important jobs. They must figure out how humans can take better care of the planet we inhabit.

Much of the work in environmental science can be explained in two ways. Some environmental scientists solve problems. Other environmental scientists prevent problems.

Environmental scientists who solve problems look for ways to clean up the "messes" humans are already making, like hazardous waste and pollution.

Environmental scientists working to prevent problems look for earth-friendly solutions and alternative ways of getting things done with fewer resources. Simply using less packaging for soaps or cereal boxes not only means there's less trash for landfills, it also takes fewer materials to make them and requires less fuel to transport them. Sometimes small changes make a big difference. Imagine what would happen if everyone

Ask Big Questions!

What can aspiring environmental scientists—kids like you!—do now to protec the earth? Here's a hint: Think "reduce, recycle, and reuse." Use your imagination, and be specific! Then put your ideas into action by raiding your family's recycling bin. Pull out a tin can, glass jar, or othe interesting object and make something totally new out of it.

used reusable shopping bags at grocery stores. It would make a huge dent in the 1 trillion bags that people around the world use and discard every year.

Some environmental problems require incredibly complicated solutions. Lots of work is being done to find alternative energy sources, like harnessing low-carbon energy from ocean tides, waves, and currents. Environmental scientists are also trying to find fuel sources that don't cause as much pollution as gasoline and oil.

There are plenty of opportunities for smart scientists with innovative ideas. Environmental scientists are more important than ever in helping ensure a greener future.

Explore Some More!

You'll find free games, adventures, and movies about sustainability at **www.olliesworld.com**.

Air pollution is just one of the challenges waiting for future environmental scientists to solve.

Food Scientist

Surf the 'Net!

Search for information about some of your favorite **food brands**. **Hershey's**, anyone?

Who says you can't have your cake and eat it too? **Food scientists** use chemistry, microbiology, engineering, and scientific know-how to produce, process, present, evaluate, and distribute food. In other words, they get to play with their food!

Think of how many people love food (everyone!) and how often they like to eat it (every day!). There can be only one logical conclusion: The food industry is huge! Getting all that food from farms to grocery shelves offers amazing opportunities for food scientists.

Some food scientists work for processing companies that turn raw foods into beverages, cereals, snacks, and convenience foods. Other food scientists work in laboratories, test kitchens, and production lines to research ways to improve the nutritional value, taste, and safety of foods. They may even invent new foods.

Sometimes food scientists take ideas that have been around for a long time and make them even better. For instance, biotechnology has been used to improve foods like cheese, bread, wine, and yogurt for thousands of years. Different enzymes and microorganisms are used to make these foods taste better and last longer.

Today food scientists use biotechnology to improve the quality of agricultural crops. They hope to find ways for farmers to grow enough nutritional food to feed the world's growing population. Food scientists

Ask Big Questions!

Next time you eat a prepackaged snack, read the ingredients label. **What are all those chemicals, and why are they in our food?** See if you can recreate your favorite packaged food by making up a recipe that uses only "real" food ingredients.

Explore Some More!

Experiment with the science of cooking at **www.exploratorium.edu/cooking**.

experiment with **GMOs**, or **genetically modified organisms,** to improve the ways crops are grown. Doing this safely is a big challenge for today's food scientists.

Food scientists have already made a difference in the way the world eats. They find new and better ways to keep food fresh and safe to eat. Nutrition would be a guessing game without the information provided by food scientists.

Of course, no one has figured out how to make broccoli taste as good as candy yet. Maybe that will be your first job assignment as a food scientist! Think of the exciting opportunities waiting for future food scientists.

Can you imagine all the food scientists it takes to get food from farms to your grocery store?

Hydrologist

Surf the 'Net!

See what you can find out about your local **water supply**. Be sure to include the name of your **city** and **state** in your search.

Some places have too much. Some places have too little. It gives life, but it also kills. What is it? Water! That wet and wonderful substance also known as H_2O.

A whopping 71 percent of the earth's surface is covered in water. Water is found in, on, and above the earth.

Everyone knows liquid water is found in oceans, lakes, and rivers. But did you know water also exists below ground? It's called groundwater, and it is found in wells and porous rocks. Of course, there's also water vapor in clouds and fog.

With all that water floating around it is hard to believe there are places around the world where there isn't enough to water crops. But this is true. In some places there isn't enough to meet basic human needs for drinking, washing, and using the toilet.

There may be, as the saying goes, "water, water everywhere." But getting enough water where it is needed most gets tricky, especially when Mother Nature keeps everyone guessing by sending floods to some regions and droughts to others. Then there's pollution, **hazardous waste**, and land development and all the havoc those problems cause.

Hydrologists deal with water challenges in many ways. They look for creative ways to recycle water used in homes and farms. They design dams and irrigation systems that help communities make the most of their water supplies. They work in hydropower plants where water

Ask Big Questions!

Where does the water in your neighborhood come from? Find out where your city wastewater treatment facility is located and make a map showing how it gets from its source to your house.

is used to make power. Their job is to produce enough electricity to supply more than 1 billion homes with power.

Hydrologists also look at ways to make better use of new water sources. Figuring out a safe and affordable way to get salt out of ocean water would solve a lot of water supply problems.

Wastewater, as in the stuff people flush, is another problem hydrologists solve. They work at **wastewater** treatment facilities where dirty water is cleaned up for reuse.

Should you one day decide to become a hydrologist, you can help take care of one of the earth's most precious natural resources.

Explore Some More!

Fill your brain with H_2O at **www.epa.gov/watersense/kids/games.html**.

What happens when you flush? The wastewater moves through sewage systems to be treated by hydrologists at plants like this.

Marine Biologist

Surf the 'Net!

Search for **World Register of Marine Species (WoRMS)** to explore some of your favorite types of marine species.

Grab a windbreaker, slip on your deck shoes, and hop aboard the research ship. It's time to get work! The ocean is your laboratory. You are a marine biologist and today you'll observe your clients in their natural habitat. First up? A **superpod** of dolphins!

What? You can get paid to work with dolphins? Yep. And sea turtles. Crocodiles and sharks too. **Marine biologists** study everything from gigantic blue whales to microbial picoplankton. No matter how big or small, every life form has its place in the ecosystem. Issues like **climate change**, **pollution**, and **endangered species** provide many opportunities where marine biologists make a difference.

Not all marine biologists actually spend their days on exciting ocean-bound expeditions. Some are found scuba diving, looking for exotic sea creatures in coral reefs. Others work in deep ocean waters in submersible vessels. Still others work at aquariums or zoos. Marine biologists observe marine life in and out of natural habitats.

Marine biologists typically spend more time on land than at sea. There are data to be analyzed, satellites to monitor, samples to study, computer models to build. Important work is done in laboratories, where marine biologists conduct research, study specimens, and write reports. Time in the lab is where they reflect on what they have seen at sea.

Ask Big Questions!

What type of marine species are in danger of becoming extinct? Use the Internet and library resources to learn more. Use the information you discover to create a poster to inspire other people to focus on solutions for the problem.

Explore Some More!

Dive in and discover ocean expeditions with the Woods Hole Oceanographic Institute at **www.divediscover.whoi.edu**.

One recent expedition involved exploring extreme, hostile environments found deep underwater in the Pacific Ocean hundreds of miles off the coast of Manzanillo, Mexico. This is where researchers found microbes, crabs, and giant tubeworms surviving in the warm water next to searing hot hydrothermal vents. Marine biologists spent weeks actually exploring the ocean. They spent many months in the lab working with the data and samples they collected.

As many as one million species live in the world's oceans. Between one-third and two-thirds of those species are yet to be named and described. What will the next wave of marine biologists discover?

Imagine swimming with sea creatures like these.

Veterinarian

True or false? **Veterinarians** love animals. The answer, as you can easily guess, is a big, enthusiastic true!

Veterinarians are specially trained doctors who take care of sick or injured animals. In fact, veterinarians know as much about animals as your family doctor knows about people. Diagnosing problems can be a little trickier for veterinarians though. Their patients cannot talk to tell the doctor where it hurts or how they feel.

Surf the 'Net!

Take a virtual visit to the National Zoo in Washington, D.C., and watch animals on its animal web cams.

Some diseases are easier to detect than others. Did you know animals, like humans, get complex diseases such as cancer, diabetes, and depression?

In America alone, the Humane Society estimates about 164 million households have at least one pet. And, get this—all these families spend billions of dollars every year feeding and caring for their pets.

Most of these pets visit a veterinarian for checkups at least once a year. Pet care alone keeps many vets very busy. These doctors use their knowledge—and good detective skills—to care for pets like dogs, cats, and birds. These vets work in clinics, where they see both healthy and sick animals for all kinds of reasons.

Just like doctors who work with humans, vets spend a lot of time keeping healthy pets healthy. They give immunizations to prevent diseases, and they give advice about exercise and diet. Regular checkups help veterinarians spot problems early on, when treatment is more effective.

Ask Big Questions!

Adopting a pet is a big responsibility. **What do people need to think about before bringing an animal into their home?** Make a pet care to-do list for your family's pet. If you do not have a pet, visit the website of your local animal shelter and print out the picture of the pet you would choose. Make up a pet care to-do list for your imaginary pet.

Large animal vets care for animals on farms and ranches. They tend to horses, cows, sheep, and other farm animals. Some veterinarians specialize in working with racehorses or reptiles like snakes and turtles. Still other veterinarians work at zoos. Some even run away with the circus and treat a wide variety of animals while traveling all over the country.

Some veterinarians conduct research to find new medicines for sick animals. Others work with pet food companies devising tasty new blends of pet chow.

There are many ways for people who love animals to help their feathered and furry friends stay healthy and happy.

Explore Some More!

Download the free Animal Hospital video game at **www.avma.org/KB/K12/videogame/index.html**.

Anything that a family doctor does for humans, a veterinarian does for animals.

Find *Your* Future in Science

Let's review the amazing career ideas you've just discovered. Below are descriptions of some of the opportunities waiting for people who like science. Read them and see if you can match them with the correct job titles.

Please do not write in this book. Use a separate sheet of paper to write your answers and imagine your future! Or, even better, go online to download a free activity sheet at www.cherrylakepublishing.com/activities.

- A Astrophysicist
- B Chemist
- C Crime scene investigator
- D Environmental scientist
- E Food scientist
- F Hydrologist
- G Marine biologist
- H Veterinarian

1. Performs lifesaving surgery on a family's beloved pet
2. Explores ways marine organisms can be used in lifesaving medicines
3. Protects endangered animal species from extinction
4. Plans manned missions to Mars, the moon, and other extraterrestrial destinations
5. Eliminates bad hair days with a foolproof styling gel
6. Solves the crime of the century
7. Develops a way to make broccoli taste as good as candy
8. Eliminates water poverty around the world

(Answer Key: 1-H; 2-G; 3-D; 4-A; 5-B; 6-C; 7-E; 8-F)

Glossary

astrophysicist scientist who studies celestial objects, space, and the universe

chemist person who studies or does research in the science of chemistry, which is the science of all matter that can be touched, seen, felt, or smelled

climate change a change in global or regional climate patterns that some scientists believe are caused by increased levels of atmospheric carbon dioxide produced by the use of fossil fuels

crime scene investigator person who processes crime scenes and forensic evidence

deoxyribonucleic acid (DNA) a molecule with instructions that tell cells what their jobs are

endangered species species of animal or planet in danger of extinction due to human activity, changes in weather, or other factors

environmental scientist person who uses science to solve environmental problems like pollution

food scientist person who uses his or her knowledge of chemistry, biochemistry, microbiology, and engineering to convert grain, livestock, fruit, and vegetables into new food products

forensics scientific tests or techniques used in the investigation of crime

galaxy one of the many very large systems of stars, gas, and dust that make up the universe

genetically modified organism (GMO) plants, animals, or microorganisms in which the genetic material has been altered in a way that does not occur naturally

hydrologist scientist who deals with the movement, distribution, and quality of water

marine biologist scientist who works with marine organisms

pollution the introduction of contaminants into the natural environment that cause adverse change

satellite a device launched to orbit around the earth, moon, or another planet to collect information or aid communication

superpod a large school or herd of whales and dolphins

septillion a cardinal number represented in the United States by 1s followed by 24 zeros

sustainable practices that do not completely use up or destroy natural resources

telescope an optical instrument for making distant objects appear larger and nearer

veterinarian doctor who takes care of animal patients

wastewater water that has been used in washing, flushing, manufacturing, and other purposes

Index

About the Author

Diane Lindsey Reeves is the author of lots of children's books. She has written several original PEANUTS stories (published by Regnery Kids and Sourcebooks). She is especially curious about what people do and likes to write books that get kids thinking about all the cool things they can be when they grow up. She lives in Cary, North Carolina and her favorite thing to do is play with her grandkids—Conrad, Evan, Reid, and Hollis Grace.